SOULS IN STONE

SOULS IN STONE

European Graveyard Sculpture

PHOTOGRAPHED BY

Anne de Brunhoff

With an Introduction by Thomas B. Hess

Alfred A. Knopf   New York   1978

THIS IS A BORZOI BOOK PUBLISHED BY ALFRED A. KNOPF, INC.

Copyright © 1978 by Anne de Brunhoff
Introduction Copyright © 1978 by Alfred A. Knopf, Inc.
All rights reserved under International and Pan-American Copyright Conventions. Published in the United States by Alfred A. Knopf, Inc., New York, and simultaneously in Canada by Random House of Canada Limited, Toronto. Distributed by Random House, Inc., New York.

Library of Congress Cataloging in Publication Data
Brunhoff, Anne de [date].   Souls in stone.

1. Sepulchral monuments—France.   2. Sepulchral monuments, Victorian—France.
3. Sepulchral monuments—Italy.   4. Sepulchral monuments, Victorian—Italy.   I. Title.
NB1865.B78   1978   730'.945   77-20371
ISBN 0-394-73283-9

Grateful acknowledgment is made for the following reproduction rights:

Page viii, Giorgio de Chirico, *The Enigma of a Day* (1914). Oil on canvas, 72¾″ x 55½″.
Collection, James Thrall Soby, New Canaan.

Page ix, René Magritte, *Souvenir de Voyage* (1955). Oil on canvas, 63⅞″ x 51¼″. Collection, the Museum of Modern Art, New York. Gift of D. and J. de Menil.

Page x, Umberto Boccioni, *Unique Forms of Continuity in Space* (1913). Bronze (cast 1931), 43⅞″ x 34⅞″ x 15¾″. Collection, the Museum of Modern Art, New York. Acquired through the Lillie P. Bliss Bequest.

Manufactured in the United States of America
FIRST EDITION

INTRODUCTION

The triumph of modernist public sculpture in the second half of the twentieth century also signals the defeat of late nineteenth- and early-twentieth-century realist Beaux-Arts monumental styles. For every Alexander Calder or Henry Moore that rears its head above the snarling traffic ramps in Amsterdam or Grand Rapids, you can assume that somehow, someplace, a nationalist general or laissez-faire tycoon, cast slightly over life size in bronze as tender as clotted cream, has been pulled down from its granite plinth. André Malraux, always a few minutes ahead of his time in ministerial decisions, about fifteen years ago removed the jigging nymphs and importunate satyrs from the gardens of the Carrousel and substituted a complete set of mighty Maillol nudes. Only after they had disappeared did a few poets begin to regret the abandoned works which had taught generations of *flâneurs* the lessons of classicism, eroticism, and kitsch.

It is as if there were an economics of sculpture at work, and at any given time only a certain number of monuments can stand as functions of the collective yearning. In order to hasten the change from the old order, modernist artists, critics, dealers, decorators, and publicists were eager to deride the old pieties, just as, in their prime, the academicians deplored and blackguarded every sort of modernist proposal, *ad hominem, ad rem, ad astra per nauseam.* The Greco-Roman canons of nude beauty, elegant drapery, theatrical gesture, within appropriate architectural frameworks, were denounced and defended with equal vigor.

Recently it would seem that the moderns have been consolidating a victory. The memorials our grandparents, with touching optimism, dedicated to eternity at the crossroads of every nascent urban sprawl and blight are mockingly abandoned. The Beaux-Arts sculptors stand accused of the crimes of nonfunctionalism, eclecticism, and systematic impurity. Their forms, it seems, do not articulate the materials from which they were made or the physical laws that keep them from falling down; they are apt to seem something they are not; and they are riddled with anecdote, literature, idiot-savant allusions. The public is urged to laugh at these bronze and marble foibles, as if the official monuments of today, by Lipchitz, Moore, Manzù, and others, are so much better.

History and historians take the longer, calmer view. After all, the great Auguste Rodin was shamefully neglected only thirty years ago by avid formalists who felt that his illusionist use of shadows and deep modeling, his fluent touch in wet clay, his satin-smooth marbles betrayed certain glyptic verities that were recovered, just in time, by Constantin Brancusi and his mystique of direct carving. Only lately has Rodin regained his position as the formidable, Janus-faced demiurge who closes the time of palaces and opens the age of anxiety. Academic painters, too, from the proto-feminist Rosa Bonheur to the proto-Surrealist Arnold Böcklin, are being seriously restudied by scholars always in need of new Ph.D. dissertation topics as well as by dealers in search of fresh inventory and by collectors bargain hunting. And, you should add, by the mass public which never fell out of love with the trompe-l'oeil magic of naturalism or accepted the hegemony of modernist line, color, and form. As for academic sculpture, you can be sure that the cemeteries of Milan and Genoa, the parks of Philadelphia and Rome, the boulevards of Paris and Turin are being explored by platoons of graduate students on the hunt for new names, forgotten monuments, and valuable footnotes.

The beauty, ingenuity, and virtuosity evident in the sculptures and monuments photographed by de Brunhoff in cemeteries in northern Italy, Paris and environs, and the Ile de Ré indicate something of the rewards available to patient connoisseurs with an eye for the glitter of originality.

The mighty civic monuments, with their generous budgets, of course attracted the most famous artists. Cemeteries included more modest enterprises, workshops suitable for lesser talents as well as for comparatively grandiose private schemes. In other words, the cemeteries documented by Anne de Brunhoff's telling photographs have sociological as well as aesthetic significance. They offer a cross section of the artistic, economic, and general cultural levels available to middle-class aspirations—a *tranche de mort*, if you will. She has discovered some primitive masonic figures in the Ile de Ré; they have the sleek stiffness of the caryatids by that more famous naïf, the postman Cheval. And there is the ultra-primitivism of Epstein's figures for the tomb of Oscar Wilde in Père Lachaise. Between the two extremes, which meet in one archaic smile, coexist every sort of mode, method, scale, and convention known to two thousand years of European craftsmanship in carving stone and casting bronze.

Especially inventive are the architectural fantasies; the hillside in the Camposanto in Genoa looks an like excavation in which chapels, mosques, temples, and tiny cathedrals of every age and condition are piled on top of one another in crazy archaeological perspective. A peculiar late-twentieth-century view of history is predicted in such mélanges, a creative eclecticism that has been called Post-Modern. The stance assumes that everything that is known is equally available and valid, so long as it looks good; you can insert a Gothic sprocket on a Romanesque vault between Egyptian piers with Rococo moldings for Art Deco patterns if you want. And it's not simply a matter of style. In the reduced scale of a crypt, architecture can submit to the most melodramatic collages. And "follies." Usually a visionary building stays on the drawing boards; it's too expensive for clients and architects. The masterpieces of Boullée, for example, and Lequeu, never were realized. For a family tomb, however, almost anything goes. At Père Lachaise there are little gems by Labrouste and Viollet-le-Duc. Lenoir's Tomb of Eloise and Abélard—a fairy-tale bit of petrified fiction—probably contains some bits and pieces of original sculpture and architectural members from the royal cathedral of St. Denis.

Elsewhere statues proliferate with such remarkable energy that it's hard to accept the idea that they were part of a dying tradition, that these are the moribund remnants of an adventure begun by the Pisanos and Donatello five hundred years before. The art is public, epic. The mourners call their grief to the heavens. Homeric sorrows, tragic losses, rivers of tears, lips quivering with sobs. But something has gone wrong. The pathos is too heavy for the shapes that are designed to contain it. Images keep sliding into theater and, below theater, to the *tableau vivant* or the charade. Context is lost along with scale and a logical grammar of forms.

Isn't this sense of losses, in a way, appropriate to the funerary? The artist longs for

the grand statement just as a son longs for his father or the marquise for her poodle. And at this point—at the intersection of intentional art and art in spite of itself—the Surrealist aspects of late-nineteenth- and early-twentieth-century academic sculpture are sensed at their keenest. It was Giorgio de Chirico, I suppose—that brilliant pedestrian and connoisseur of Turin streets—and after him René Magritte, who recognized the strange poetry of a granite top hat held by a figure in a granite frock coat with granite buttonholes and granite shoelaces. Oedipus' nightmare of the avenging father is turned to implacable stone. In de Chirico's *The Enigma of a Day*, 1914 (Fig. 1), the statue presides over a railroad station plaza filled with the melancholy of departures. In Magritte's *Memory of a Voyage*, 1955 (Fig. 2), he is the monster who came and, like Mozart's Commendatore, stayed for eternal dinner. In A. Rivalta's monument for the Drago family, in Genoa, he lounges against a doorjamb, his derby hat politely held behind his back. In G. Moreno's group, also in Genoa, he clasps his head in grief. In a jazz-age version, by C. Fait for Giuseppe Tonino, in Turin, he turns up the back of his collar and pulls his soft-brim hat down against the winds from Lethe, while puffing at a cigarette.

The facts of modern life find embodiment in traditional sculpture only through such irrational juxtapositions. "How great and poetic we are in our neckties and our patent leather boots," exclaimed Baudelaire, in 1845. And he urged contemporary artists to forge an imagery for the absolutely modern man. A few did achieve the synthesis: Manet in the flattened body and level glance of a young prostitute, Seurat in a Sundy afternoon promenade as stately as the ceremonies of the Sung emperors, Rodin in the *Gate of Hell*—except Rodin reverted to the formulas of the classic nude (Manet's *Olympia* is naked). Rodin abolished cravats and shoelaces as did many of the cemetery artists, especially when confronted with the problem of finding some new life in the old mythologies. The rubbery athlete on a tomb in Milan, grappling with a propeller in front of a horrified, decapitated Medusa, presumably reenacts, for a World War I pilot, Perseus' feat, with a biplane as Pegasus, plus a tag from d'Annunzio. The image is so freighted with caricatural modeling and distortion—elongations aren't always elegant—that it collapses under its own rhetoric ("deflates" is perhaps a better verb). The piece might be grotesque; it's by no means stupid.

Fig. 2

Notice how cleverly the figure's elevated right leg is cantilevered by the prop. Note, too, the allusions to the Victory of Samothrace and to that other, nobly windblown, striding figure, Umberto Boccioni's *Unique Forms of Continuity in Space,* 1913 (Fig. 3). Indeed its closeness to Boccioni in patriotic fervor as well as athletic posture indicates how surprisingly easy it was for avant-garde ideas to filter down to the bourgeois vernacular of the Camposanto.

Traditionalism could be a strength as well as a weakness. The sheer ability of the French to cut and build with Ile-de-France stone shines through many otherwise stereotyped monuments at Père Lachaise and Montmartre. The buttresses of Notre Dame and the pilasters of the Invalides inform the work of these modest, skilled quarriers and masons. In Italy they drilled marble and cast bonze as if the obdurate materials were butter. And the tradition of the "beautiful child" lasted until Mussolini's socialist-realist dogmatics. The thoughtful angel Gabriel that guards Giulio Monteverde's monument for the Oneto family of Genoa, with its learned contrasts of soft and hard textures (gauze robe, brass trumpet, feather wings, adolescent flesh) and, above all, the reticence and precision of its play of vertical with diagonal lines and arcs, is a modest link in the chain that goes back to Canova's Neo-Classicism, and beyond him to Bernini, Luca della Robbia, and Donatello. A mantle of grime covers the upper arms of the figure, as if to symbolize the neglect and contempt with which such statues are treated nowadays. Ironically, it adds a touch of drama to an otherwise perfunctory modeling as well as a token of the real within a rather frigid idealism. Such are some of the virtues of benign neglect. As in the Debarbieri-Pozzo monument by L. Brizzolara, in Genoa, a patina of mysterious, rippling glamour—shuttling, flickering—comes from deposits of superficial soot and dirt.

Some of the charm of these photographs is a product of filters, physical and metaphysical: the green and orange glass ones that fit over the camera's lens, the fuzzy ones of nostalgia that blur the mind's eye. Many of the pieces that once looked dreadful have lapsed, with time, into comfortable quaintness. Pretensions that must have seemed brutal when they had the power of money and guns behind them now look merely human—frail and human. And the photographer's skill is there to cover a gaffe with shadows or to

Fig. 3

P. 65

emphasize felicitous dapples of sunlight across time worn stone. Still, much of the miniature architectures seem above such accidents of taste. Giuseppe Boni's Ionic shrine for the Bocconis of Milan, for example, is an inventive solution to the question of how do you make an entablature turn a corner. Allessandro Minali's Stations of the Cross for the Bernocchi monument, also in Milan, seems to rework the helical band of Trajan's column with an eye on Tatlin's *Monument to the Third International*—a remarkable feat of proto-Post-Modern syncretism. Elsewhere abstract monsters crouch above Art Deco sarcophagus shapes to enclose a seductive nymph. The cemetery was a permissive school for builders in which anything was possible except a monumental scale, except a deployment of architectural volumes.

De Brunhoff looks at the sculptures and tombs in cemeteries the way an artist looks at nature—the way Joseph Cornell looked at similar monuments in Union Square—with an eye for the picturesque and the evocative. It's a useful service. She helps you see works that were invisible, lost behind the spectacles of high style and good taste. Now it's time to look at the works for themselves—and the sculptors, architects, and designers, too. They merit honor for their efforts and for their achievements, no matter how modest. If you laugh at them or smile in a patronizing way, you betray their humanity, and your own. To paraphrase Santayana, those who ignore old sculptures are fated to reorder them.

Thomas B. Hess

SOULS IN STONE

4

8

10

LEGÒ IL SUO COSPICUO PATRIMONIO
A FAVORE DEGLI ASILI INFANTILI
DI MILANO E DELL'OSPITALE DI VARESE

LA RICONOSCENZA DEGLI UOMINI
LA BENEDIZIONE DI DIO
LA SUA TOMBA

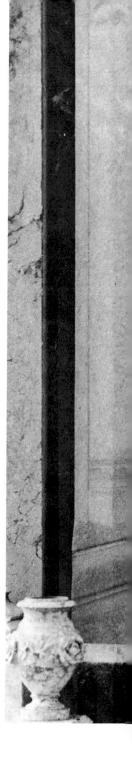

34

FAMILLE
KAMIENSKI

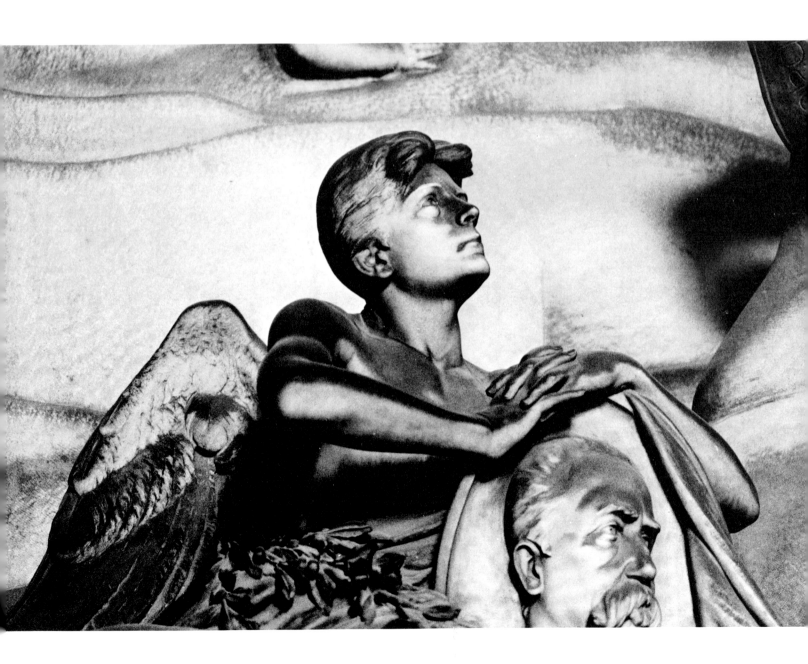

ONETO
1878

ONETO
1884

ONETO
1901

A AETERNA

GIOLINA BE
1827 ·

FRANCESC
1882 ·

LUISA DUFOU
1857 ·

ERIT IVSTVS

FRANCESCO ON
1812 — 18
LILINA   ON
1881 —
GIUSEPPE ONET
1832 — 1901

IN MEMORIA AETE

ANNIE LAVAGNINO ONE
1885 — 1972

NGIOLINA BECCHIₓONET
1827 — 1913
FRANCESCO ONETO
1882 — 1918
LUISA DUFOUR ᵥₑᴅ.ONET
1857 — 1944

ERIT IVSTVS   SALMO III

EM. ARRIGO LAVAGNINO
1884 — 1963

"AUX MÂNES
de Louis Sébastien
GOURLOT,
décédé à l'âge de 38 ans le I Avril
1816.
CE MONUMENT
fut élevé par sa veuve désolée,
dont cette statue représente les traits.
Etrangère, éloignée de sa famille,
elle a juré de ne jamais quitter la terre
hospitalière où elle trouva le bonheur
et perdit l'objet de son éternel
AMOUR.
Elle s'est réservé une place à côté
de son époux pour lui être à
jamais réunie.
Sensibles [françaises!]
vous, qui...
époux adoré...
l'étrangère...
Priez pour
SON AME."

AUX MANES
DE LOUIS SÉBASTIEN
GOURLOT
DÉCÉDÉ A L'ÂGE DE 38 ANS LE 1 AVRIL
1816
CE MONUMENT

PLATES

Frontispiece: Carlo Raggio family, 1872, Genoa, Italy. Sculptor: A. Rivalta